CD-ROM
FACT*finders*
INTERACTIVE MULTIMEDIA

BIBLE STORIES

Written by
Carol Watson

Designed by
Ross Thomson

Illustrated by
Kim Woolley

Contents

The Bible lands

In Bible times, the world was very different from how it is today. Many of the countries and cities we know now didn't exist, or had different names. This map shows you how the world was then. Look at the map on page 38 to see what the Bible lands are like today.

> The mighty Roman Empire spread across many Bible lands in New Testament times (see page 24).

> Olive oil lamps were used for lighting. People also used olive oil for cooking, cleaning, and medicine.

Rome

MACEDONIA

ITALY

Phili
Thessalonica

SICILY

> The Ancient Greeks conquered many countries. They spread the Greek language and way of life to the Bible lands.

Corinth · At

GREECE

CRETE

Great Sea (Old Testament)
Mediterranean Sea (New Testament)

Houses

Most Bible lands were hot places, so homes were built to keep out the heat. Houses had flat roofs and small windows. Inside the house it was cool and shady.

> The Ancient Egyptians were very powerful in Old Testament times (see page 12). Their kings were called pharaohs, and they were buried in huge stone pyramids by the Nile River.

> Camels carried people and goods for long distances across the desert. They can live on poor food and go without water for several days.

> A working man wore a white, knee-length tunic. He tucked this into his belt when he worked.

Clothing

People wore long, flowing robes to keep cool. To protect their heads from the sun, they wore a turban, a piece of cloth held on with a cord.

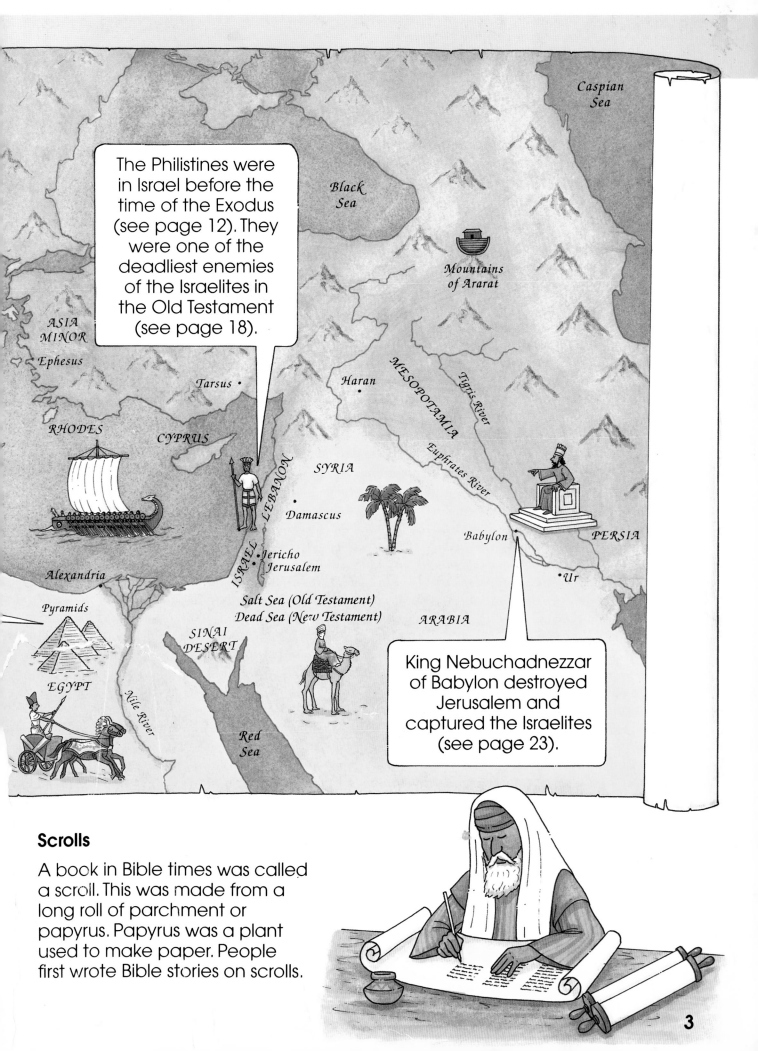

The Philistines were in Israel before the time of the Exodus (see page 12). They were one of the deadliest enemies of the Israelites in the Old Testament (see page 18).

King Nebuchadnezzar of Babylon destroyed Jerusalem and captured the Israelites (see page 23).

Scrolls

A book in Bible times was called a scroll. This was made from a long roll of parchment or papyrus. Papyrus was a plant used to make paper. People first wrote Bible stories on scrolls.

In the beginning

The Old Testament section of the Bible tells us that at the beginning of time God made the world. He created animals and birds, trees and flowers, rivers and seas. Everything that he made was wonderful. Then he created a man and a woman, called Adam and Eve, to enjoy this beautiful world.

The Garden of Eden

Adam and Eve lived happily in the Garden of Eden. In the middle of the garden were two special trees. One was called the Tree of Life. The other was called the Tree of the Knowledge of Good and Evil. God told Adam that he was not allowed to eat the fruit from this tree.

The serpent

The serpent persuaded Eve to eat some fruit from the forbidden tree. Then Eve tempted Adam to eat the fruit, too. God was angry. He cursed the serpent and sent Adam and Eve out of the Garden of Eden.

The world outside the Garden of Eden

From then on, men and women had to work hard. They could no longer eat the fruit from the Tree of Life and live forever. They also knew the difference between good and evil, and many of them chose to lead wicked lives.

Noah and the Flood

God grew more and more angry about people's wicked behavior. Finally, he decided to kill everyone in a flood. There was one good man called Noah. So God warned Noah about the flood and told him to build a huge boat, called an ark. Noah took two of every creature onto the ark with his family. Then it rained for forty days and nights, and water flooded the Earth. Everything was destroyed apart from the ark. After many months, the flood waters went down until the ark settled on the mountains of Ararat.

God's promise

God promised Noah that he would never flood the Earth again. He called this agreement his "covenant," and put a rainbow in the sky to remind people of his promise.

Noah's sons

Noah's sons, Shem, Ham, and Japheth, settled in different areas. They had children who grew up and had families of their own. These people were Noah's descendants.

5

Abraham's journey

One of Noah's descendants was a man called Terah, who lived with his family at Ur in Mesopotamia. The story of the nation of Israel begins with Terah's son, who was called Abraham.

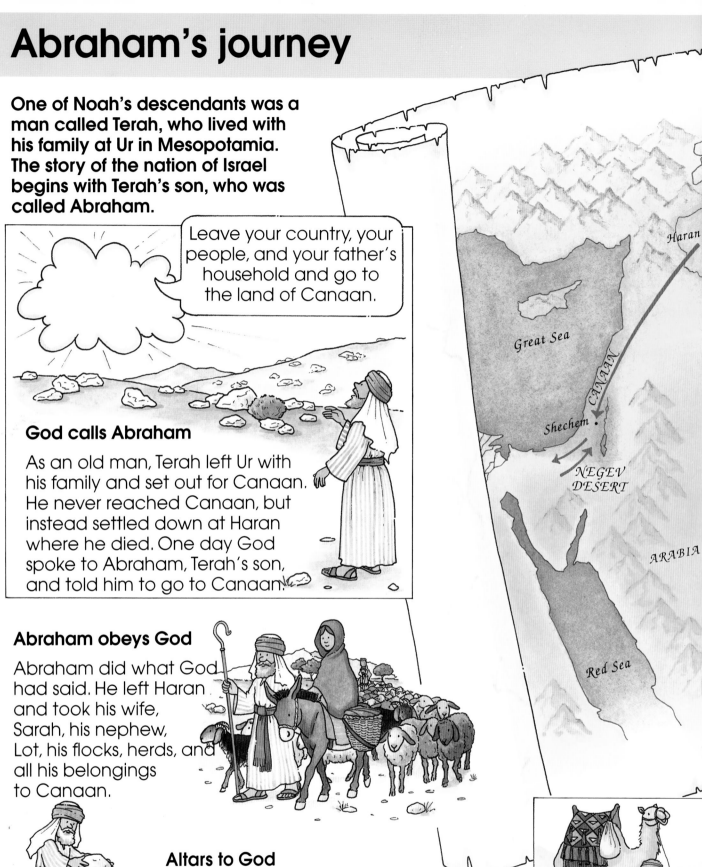

Leave your country, your people, and your father's household and go to the land of Canaan.

God calls Abraham

As an old man, Terah left Ur with his family and set out for Canaan. He never reached Canaan, but instead settled down at Haran where he died. One day God spoke to Abraham, Terah's son, and told him to go to Canaan.

Abraham obeys God

Abraham did what God had said. He left Haran and took his wife, Sarah, his nephew, Lot, his flocks, herds, and all his belongings to Canaan.

Altars to God

At Shechem and Bethel in Canaan, Abraham built altars and prayed to God. God told Abraham that he was going to give the land of Canaan to Abraham's children.

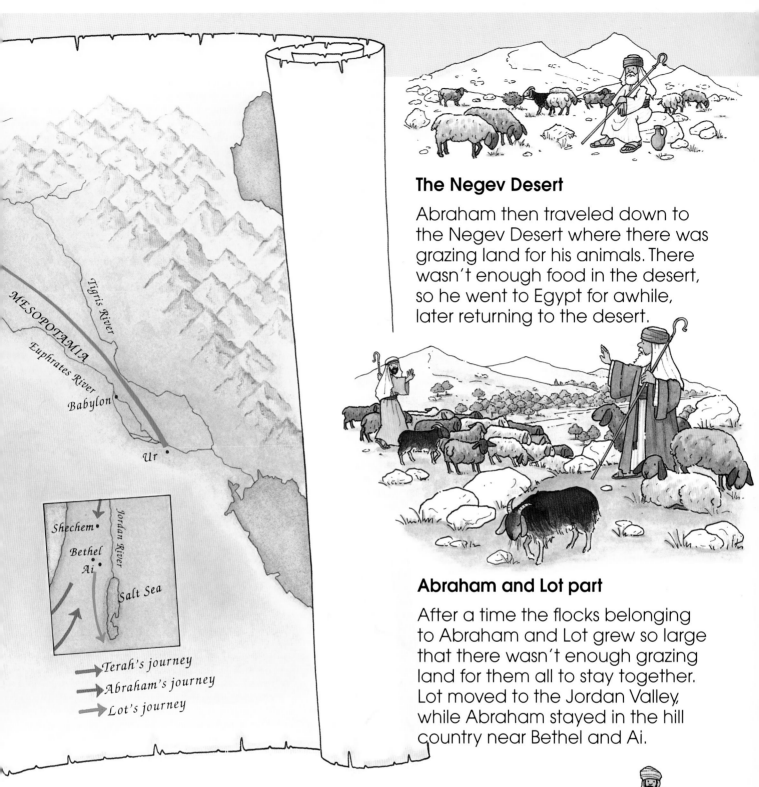

The Negev Desert

Abraham then traveled down to the Negev Desert where there was grazing land for his animals. There wasn't enough food in the desert, so he went to Egypt for awhile, later returning to the desert.

Abraham and Lot part

After a time the flocks belonging to Abraham and Lot grew so large that there wasn't enough grazing land for them all to stay together. Lot moved to the Jordan Valley, while Abraham stayed in the hill country near Bethel and Ai.

MESOPOTAMIA

Tigris River

Euphrates River

Babylon

Ur

Shechem

Bethel

Ai

Jordan River

Salt Sea

→ *Terah's journey*

→ *Abraham's journey*

→ *Lot's journey*

Nomads

Most people live in permanent homes, but nomads are people who move around the countryside taking their homes with them or building new ones wherever they stop. Abraham and his family were nomads, traveling from place to place to find grazing land for their flocks of cattle, sheep, and goats. Their animals produced meat and milk for them to eat and drink.

For a long time Abraham and Sarah had no children. Then God blessed Sarah, and when she was quite old, she had a son, called Isaac.

> Abraham, do not kill Isaac. Now I know that you are obedient to me. I will bless you. You will have as many descendants as there are stars in the sky.

Sacrifices

To make a "sacrifice" means to give up something that is precious to you. In Bible times people killed animals and offered them to God as a sacrifice. They did this to thank God or please him.

God tests Abraham

Isaac was very precious to Abraham. God tested Abraham's obedience by asking him to sacrifice Isaac. So Abraham took Isaac to a deserted place, but just as he was about to kill his son, God spoke to him.

Isaac and Rebekah

When Isaac grew up, he married a beautiful woman called Rebekah. She came from the land where Abraham had been born. Isaac and Rebekah had twin sons, called Esau and Jacob.

Esau and Jacob

Esau was the elder of the twins, so he was due to receive the birthright and blessing from their father, Isaac. Jacob was jealous of Esau, so with the help of his mother, he tricked Esau out of his birthright and blessing.

Haran

Tigris River

MESOPOTAMIA

Great Sea

Euphrates River

CANAAN

Salt Sea

→ *Jacob flees to Haran*

Birthright

The firstborn son always became head of the family after his father's death. He also inherited a double share of his father's possessions. This was called the "birthright," and with it came his father's blessing for the future.

Jacob leaves Canaan

Esau swore to kill Jacob once his father was dead. So Jacob fled to Haran to work for his uncle, who was called Laban.

Haran

MESOPOTAMIA

Tigris River

Great Sea

Euphrates River

CANAAN

Salt Sea

→ *Jacob returns to Canaan*

God blesses Jacob

After twenty years at Haran, Jacob owned huge flocks of sheep and herds of cattle and had two wives, called Rachel and Leah. They all returned to Canaan where Esau welcomed Jacob and forgave him for taking his birthright. At that time God blessed Jacob and gave him a new name, Israel.

Joseph in Egypt

Jacob settled in Canaan with his wives and their families. He had many children, but his favorites were Joseph and his baby brother, Benjamin. They were the sons of Rachel, the wife Jacob loved more.

Joseph's coat

To show how much he loved him, Jacob gave Joseph a special coat of many colors. When Joseph's older brothers saw how much Jacob favored Joseph, they were very jealous and hated him.

Joseph is sold into slavery

One day Joseph visited his brothers, who were looking after the flocks of sheep at Dothan. When they saw Joseph coming, the brothers plotted to kill him.

The spice trade

The spice trade was an important trade in Bible times. People used spices for food, incense, and makeup. The trade route from Damascus, in Syria, to Egypt ran past Dothan where Joseph's brothers sold him. The Ishmaelite spice traders were desert people descended from Abraham.

However, some Ishmaelite spice traders passed by on their way to Egypt, so the brothers sold Joseph to the traders. They took Joseph to Egypt and sold him as a slave.

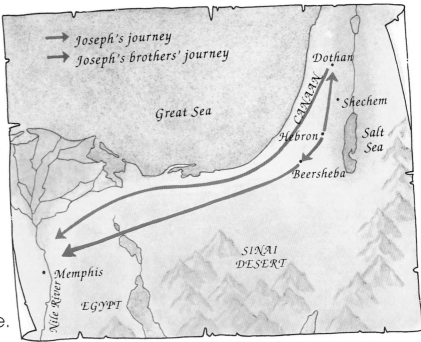

→ Joseph's journey
→ Joseph's brothers' journey

Dothan

Shechem

Great Sea

Hebron

Salt Sea

Beersheba

CANAAN

SINAI DESERT

Memphis

Nile River

EGYPT

Pharaoh's dreams

For many years Joseph worked hard and was respected by his Egyptian master. God helped Joseph to understand people's dreams, so he was able to explain the strange dreams that were worrying the Pharaoh, who was the King of Egypt.

Your dreams mean that there will be seven years of good crops followed by seven years of famine. You should store grain for this time.

The famine

The Pharaoh was so impressed with Joseph's advice that he put him in charge of all Egypt. When the famine arrived, people came to Egypt from far and wide to buy grain. Joseph's brothers came from Canaan, but they didn't recognize Joseph in his smart Egyptian clothes.

The Children of Israel

Finally, Joseph showed his brothers who he was and forgave them. They brought their old father, Jacob, and their families to live in Egypt. They were known as the Children of Israel.

Ancient Egypt

The **Nile River** was the main source of life in Egypt. If the river was high, there was water for crops, but if the river was low, it meant that the crops died and people starved.

The meaning of **dreams** was very important to people in Ancient Egypt. Wise men even wrote books to help people understand their dreams.

The escape from Egypt

Hundreds of years later, the Children of Israel had grown into a large nation. The Pharaoh at that time was cruel and forced them to work as slaves. God chose Moses to lead the Israelites out of Egypt to begin the long journey back to Canaan. This journey was called the Exodus.

God speaks to Moses

God spoke to Moses from a burning bush. He told him to ask Pharaoh to let the Israelites leave Egypt.

Moses

Moses was born in Egypt. As a baby he was put in a basket on the Nile River. He was found and cared for by Pharaoh's daughter.

I will set you free from your slavery. You will be my people, and I will be your God. I will give you a new land to live in, the land of Canaan.

Great Sea

Bitter Lakes

EGYPT

Nile River

→ *The Exodus*

Disasters and plagues

Pharaoh would not let the Israelites leave Egypt, so God sent many disasters to Egypt. There were terrible diseases, storms, and darkness as well as plagues of flies, gnats, locusts, and frogs. Water was turned into blood.

The worst disaster

Pharaoh still wouldn't listen, so God sent another disaster. One night the eldest son in every Egyptian family was killed, but God "passed over" the Israelite families, and their sons survived. At last, Pharaoh told Moses to leave Egypt.

The Passover

The Passover is a feast that the Jews still celebrate today. It reminds them of the time when God "passed over" the houses of the Israelites when they were slaves in Egypt. During the Passover, Jews eat special bread that doesn't contain any yeast.

The Israelites are chased

Moses led the Israelites to the edge of the sea where they camped. However, Pharaoh had changed his mind. His huge army was chasing the Israelites, who found themselves trapped between the Egyptian army and the sea.

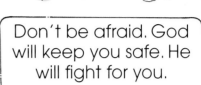

Don't be afraid. God will keep you safe. He will fight for you.

The sea divides

Moses calmed the people. He stretched his arm out over the waves, and God sent a great wind, which parted the water, making a pathway through the sea.

The Egyptians drown

The Israelites crossed the sea, and the Egyptian army chased after them. Just as the Israelites reached safe ground, God let the water pour back, and the huge Egyptian army was drowned beneath the waves. The Israelites were now free to begin their long journey through the desert.

Salt Sea

NEGEV DESERT

Kadesh Barnea

SINAI DESERT

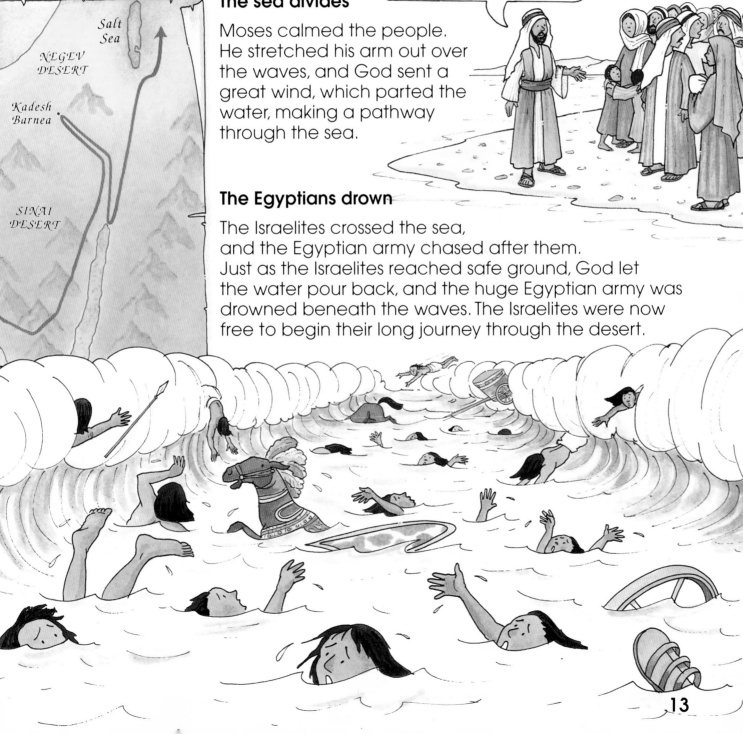

In the desert

Moses led the Israelites into the desert. They soon forgot how God had rescued them from Egypt and began to grumble about the lack of food and water. God told Moses that he would give the Israelites meat and bread to eat.

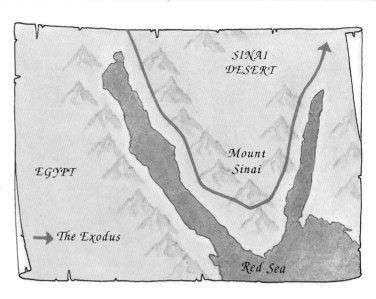

Food from God

That night a flock of quails, came down from the sky for the Israelites to eat. Then in the morning there was a layer of dew around the camp. When the dew had gone, thick frost-like flakes appeared on the ground. Moses told the people to collect this and eat it. They called it manna.

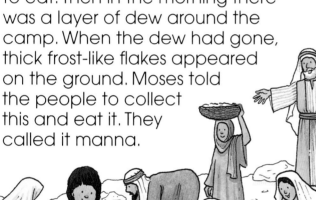

Food in the desert

Quails are small brown birds. In winter they leave Europe and fly south. Their route takes them across the desert where the Israelites were at the time of the Exodus.

Manna was white and tasted like wafers made with honey. It was the Israelites' main food during their forty years spent wandering in the desert.

Water from the rock

Moses led the Israelites on through the desert. As they grew short of water, they moaned again. Moses asked God for help, so God told Moses to strike a rock with his staff. As he did so, water appeared from the rock for the people to drink.

Mount Sinai

Months later the Israelites came to Mount Sinai. God told Moses that he would show his power to the Israelites. While Mount Sinai shook violently, they saw fire and lightning, and heard thunder and the loud blast of a trumpet. Then Moses climbed to the top of the mountain.

The Ten Commandments

God told Moses that he would be the Israelites' God if they obeyed his laws. He wrote these laws on blocks of stone and gave them to Moses. The laws were called the Ten Commandments. They were rules about the correct way for the Israelites to live their lives as God's people.

The tabernacle

God told Moses to build a large, movable tent to show the people that he was always with them. This tent was called the tabernacle. A special box, called the ark, was placed in it. This contained the Ten Commandments. The tabernacle was the holy place of God, and the ark was the holiest thing of all.

Building the tabernacle

The Israelites gave the finest things they possessed to make the tabernacle. These included fine linen, precious jewels, and beautiful embroidery.

Joshua in Canaan

After wandering in the desert for forty years, Moses led the Children of Israel to the edge of the desert. They were close to Canaan, which was the Promised Land. Moses spoke to the Israelites and warned them not to forget God once they entered Canaan.

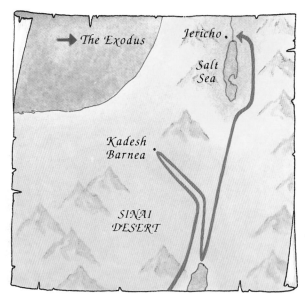

Spies enter Canaan

Moses sent men into Canaan to spy out the land. They reported back that it was a very good land, but there were large cities full of powerful people. The spies frightened the Israelites, who refused to enter Canaan. God was angry with them for not trusting that he would help them to defeat these people. As a punishment he made them wander in the desert for forty years. Moses died before they entered Canaan.

Joshua and Jericho

After the death of Moses, God called Joshua to lead the Israelites into Canaan. The first city to be captured was Jericho. This had a large wall around it, so God told Joshua what to do. Joshua's army marched around the city once a day for six days. At the front seven priests carried the ark. On the seventh day they marched around seven times, with the priests blowing trumpets made of ram's horns. The people gave a loud shout as the trumpets sounded. The walls of Jericho came crashing down, and the Israelites took the city.

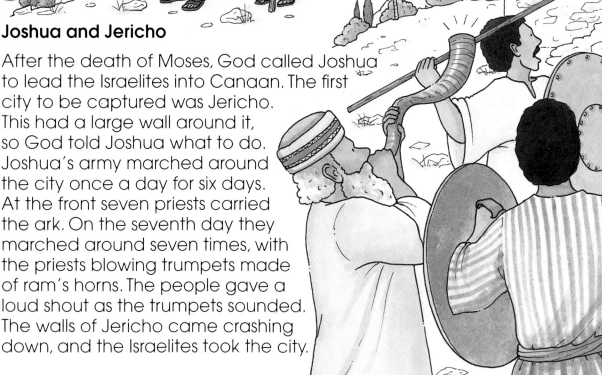

Joshua's campaigns

After capturing Jericho, Joshua's army went on to capture the main cities all over Canaan. His first campaign began in the south, at Ai. The second campaign was in the north. Joshua divided the land that his army captured among the twelve Israelite tribes.

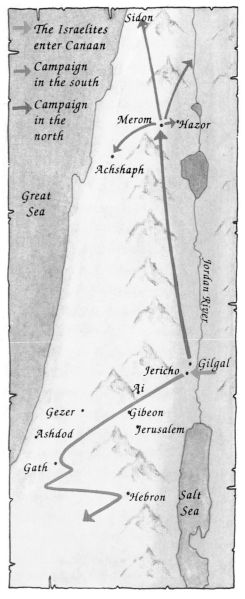

The Israelites enter Canaan

Campaign in the south

Campaign in the north

Sidon

Merom • Hazor

Achshaph

Great Sea

Jordan River

Jericho • Gilgal

Ai

Gezer • Gibeon

Ashdod Jerusalem

Gath •

• Hebron Salt Sea

King Saul

For a long time after they had settled in Canaan, the tribes of Israel had many enemies. They fought battles against fierce armies, led by powerful kings. Their most deadly enemies were the Philistines. The people of Israel decided that it was time they had their own king to lead them against their enemies. This was because they had turned away from God, and no longer thought of him as their king.

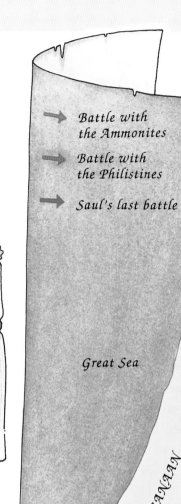

Battle with the Ammonites

Battle with the Philistines

Saul's last battle

Great Sea

CANAAN

NEGEV DESERT

Saul, the warrior king

God told Samuel to make Saul king of Israel. Samuel was a prophet, which meant he received messages from God. Saul led his army against the Ammonites and won a great victory. Then he defeated the Philistines. Saul won many battles, but he didn't always obey God. God was angry and decided that Saul should no longer be king.

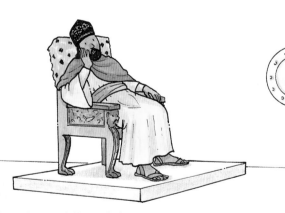

Saul and David

A shepherd boy called David was to be the next king. He went to live at Saul's court where he played music on his harp to soothe Saul's fits of depression. Saul did not know that David was the future king.

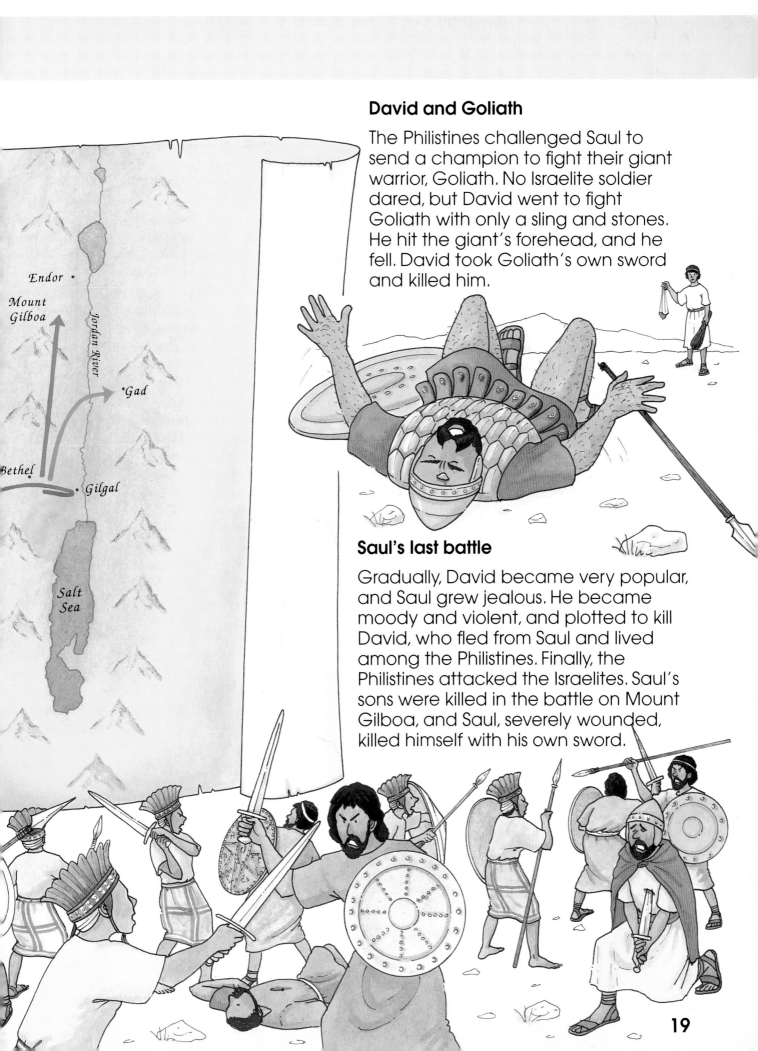

David and Goliath

The Philistines challenged Saul to send a champion to fight their giant warrior, Goliath. No Israelite soldier dared, but David went to fight Goliath with only a sling and stones. He hit the giant's forehead, and he fell. David took Goliath's own sword and killed him.

Saul's last battle

Gradually, David became very popular, and Saul grew jealous. He became moody and violent, and plotted to kill David, who fled from Saul and lived among the Philistines. Finally, the Philistines attacked the Israelites. Saul's sons were killed in the battle on Mount Gilboa, and Saul, severely wounded, killed himself with his own sword.

Endor

Mount Gilboa

Jordan River

Gad

Bethel

Gilgal

Salt Sea

19

The kingdom of David

After Saul's death David became king of Israel. The first thing he did was to capture the fortress of Jerusalem and make it his capital. He called it "the city of David."

David captures Jerusalem

The Jebusites lived in Jerusalem. They closed up the main entrance to the city and dug an underground tunnel to the water source outside the city walls. One of David's officers, called Joab, found a way into the water tunnel. He and his men traveled up the tunnel and took the city by surprise.

Jerusalem

David made Jerusalem into a city of great beauty and splendor. The work was continued by his son, Solomon. Today Jerusalem is still the capital of Israel where the government meets.

The ark comes to Jerusalem

Praise the Lord!

David made Jerusalem the holy city of Israel by taking the ark of the Lord there. The Israelites followed the ark and rejoiced. David sang praises to God and danced for joy. God promised David that his descendants would reign forever.

20

David conquers his enemies

Once David was king of Israel, the Philistines attacked him in full force. God told David to lead his army against them, and the Israelites had a great victory. David went on to defeat all his enemies, and he formed a large kingdom.

Psalms of David

David wrote many poems, called psalms, to tell God how he was feeling. Some of them are happy and full of thanks and praise. Others show that David was sometimes angry or sad. David's psalms are collected together with other psalms in the Bible.

David makes Solomon king

When David was a very old man, he promised his kingdom to his son Solomon. David told Solomon to obey God so that he would rule wisely and have a happy life.

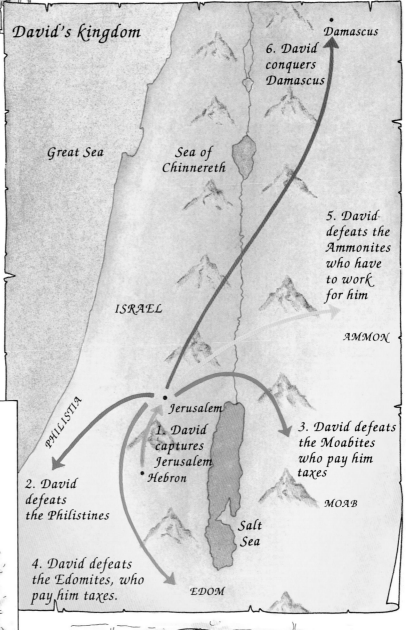

David's kingdom

Damascus

6. David conquers Damascus

Great Sea

Sea of Chinnereth

5. David defeats the Ammonites who have to work for him

ISRAEL

AMMON

PHILISTIA

Jerusalem

1. David captures Jerusalem

Hebron

3. David defeats the Moabites who pay him taxes

2. David defeats the Philistines

MOAB

Salt Sea

4. David defeats the Edomites, who pay him taxes.

EDOM

The Romans and King Herod

Four centuries later the Jewish people were once again under the control of a powerful enemy, the Romans. They had conquered Palestine (the Roman name for Canaan), and the Jews had to pay taxes to the Roman emperor. The Jews longed for freedom and wanted a savior or a king, like David, to rescue them from their troubles.

The Roman Empire

The Romans had a large army, which conquered many countries of the world. These became part of a huge empire that was ruled by the emperor in Rome, in Italy. In the years that they were powerful, there were many emperors. Augustus was the emperor at the time of Jesus's birth.

Roman soldiers

Roman soldiers wore strong armor. They marched in large groups called legions, which were divided into smaller groups of fifty to a hundred men. Each group was led by a centurion. As well as fighting battles, the soldiers kept order in the cities ruled by the Romans. There were soldiers in Jerusalem whose job was to stop riots and carry out executions.

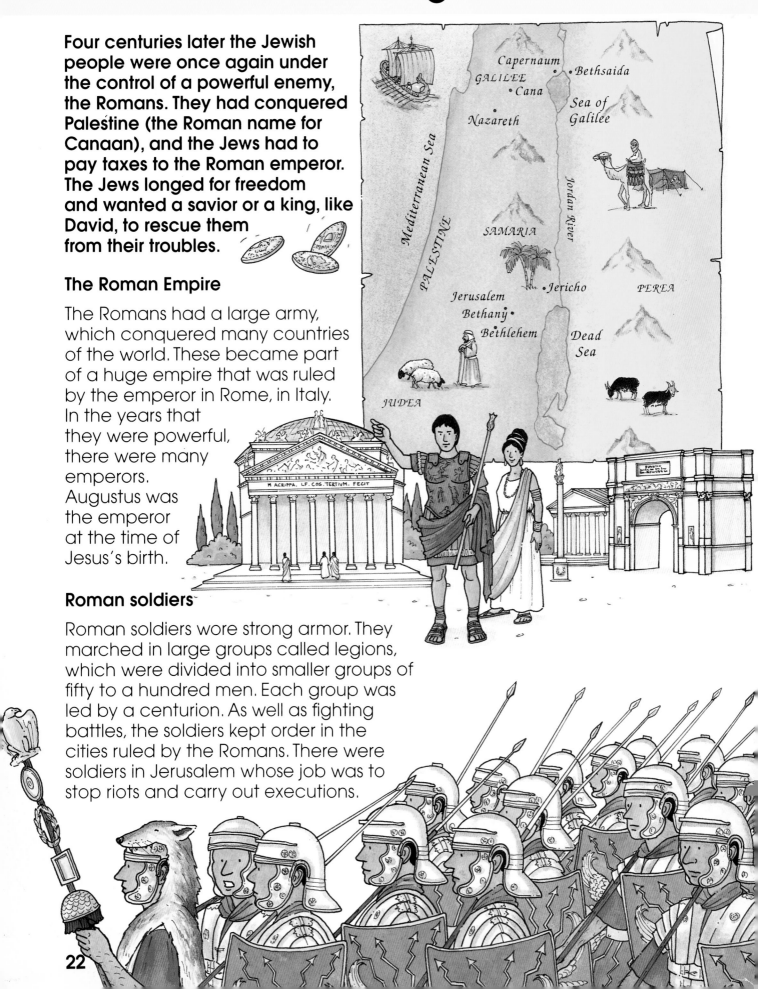

King Herod the Great

The King of the Jews at this time was Herod. He was always trying to impress the Roman emperor and built a port for Augustus's ships at Caesarea. He also built palaces and an amphitheater. Herod was allowed to rule over all of Palestine on Augustus's behalf.

The new temple

King Herod was always worried that he was going to lose his power. He tried to please his people, the Jews, by building a large new temple in Jerusalem. Herod was king at the time of Jesus's birth.

Roman developments

The Romans were famous for building straight roads all over their empire. You can still see some of these today. They also developed plumbing and central heating systems for houses.

The birth of Jesus

The New Testament section of the Bible tells us that a man called Joseph, who was a descendant of the great King David, lived in Nazareth, in Galilee. Joseph was a carpenter and worked hard for his living. He was happy because he was going to marry Mary.

> Don't be afraid, Mary. God is pleased with you. You are going to have a son who will be very special. You must call him Jesus. He will be God's promised king — the king who will reign forever.

Mary and the angel

One day when Mary was alone, a bright light filled the room, and a voice spoke to her. It was an angel, who told her that she was going to have a special baby who would be God's own son. Mary did not understand, but she promised to do what God wanted.

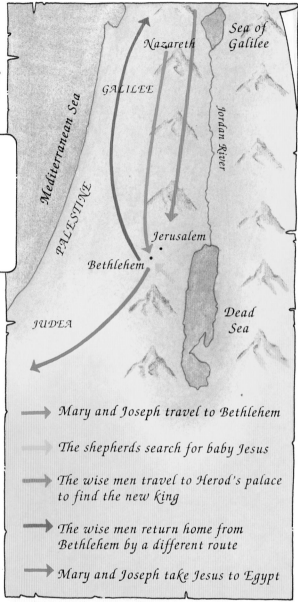

→ Mary and Joseph travel to Bethlehem

→ The shepherds search for baby Jesus

→ The wise men travel to Herod's palace to find the new king

→ The wise men return home from Bethlehem by a different route

→ Mary and Joseph take Jesus to Egypt

The journey to Bethlehem

Mary and Joseph were married. Some months later Joseph had to travel to the town of Bethlehem, which was far away in Judea. Mary made the long journey with Joseph, even though it was almost time for her baby to be born.

Jesus is born

There were so many visitors to Bethlehem that Mary and Joseph couldn't find anywhere to spend the night. At last, they found shelter in a stable. That night, among the animals, Mary's baby was born. As there was no cradle, she laid him in the manger to sleep.

The shepherds

On the hillside outside Bethlehem, there were shepherds watching over their flocks of sheep. Suddenly, a bright light lit up the sky, and an angel spoke to them, telling them about the birth of Jesus, God's promised king. The shepherds searched until they found the baby in the stable. Then they knelt down and worshiped him.

The wise men

Wise men from faraway lands in the East saw a bright new star shining in the sky. It was God's sign that a new king had been born. They told this to King Herod in Jerusalem, who decided to kill Jesus because he was frightened that Jesus would take over his throne. At last, the wise men found the house and gave Jesus expensive presents. However, they didn't tell King Herod where the baby was.

King Herod's plot

King Herod was so frightened about the birth of Jesus that he ordered all the boys under two years old to be killed. Mary and Joseph were warned about this in a dream. They escaped to Egypt, where baby Jesus was safe.

The life of Jesus

Mary and Joseph returned from Egypt to live in Nazareth, where Jesus grew up. He was waiting for the time when God wanted to use him. Jesus had a cousin, called John, who was a prophet. John told everyone that they should live their lives in the way God commanded. He also told them that God was sending someone special to them.

You are my son, and I love you.

Baptism

John the Baptist baptized people who wanted to obey God. Baptism involved covering a person with water. This was a symbol of washing away the things that the person had done wrong, so they could live their lives in a way that would please God.

John the Baptist

When people heard John speak, some of them wanted to live better lives. John baptized them in the Jordan River. When it was time for Jesus to start God's work, he left Nazareth and was baptized by John. As Jesus came out of the water, God spoke to him saying that he loved him.

Jesus calls his followers

After his baptism Jesus spent forty days in the desert where the devil tried to get him to use God's power in the wrong way. Then Jesus went to Galilee where he asked four fishermen, called Peter, Andrew, James, and John, to follow him. They were the first followers of Jesus and were known as the disciples. Later there were eight more disciples.

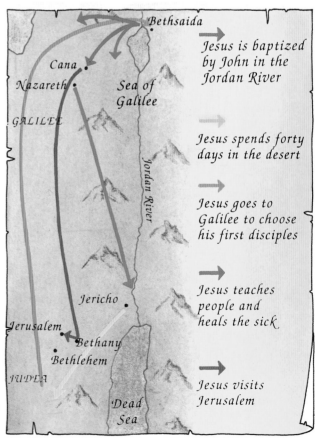

Jesus is baptized by John in the Jordan River

Jesus spends forty days in the desert

Jesus goes to Galilee to choose his first disciples

Jesus teaches people and heals the sick

Jesus visits Jerusalem

Jesus heals the sick

Jesus traveled to many places and talked to people about God. To make it easier for the crowds to understand what he was telling them, Jesus often used short stories, called parables, to explain something. Jesus also healed many sick people, some of whom had been ill for years. The news about Jesus spread far and wide, and large crowds gathered to hear him.

Miracles

Jesus also showed God's power in ways other than healing. He calmed a fierce storm and walked on water. He changed water into wine at a wedding and fed five thousand people with only two fish and five loaves of bread. These were God's signs to people that his son was on the Earth.

Jesus comes to Jerusalem

When it was time to visit Jerusalem, Jesus entered the city on a donkey. The crowds welcomed him and cheered. They waved branches of palms and spread their cloaks on the road in front of him.

Jesus rises from the dead

In Jerusalem, Jesus continued his teaching. Each day crowds of people came to hear him speak outside the temple. The Jewish chief priests became angry because Jesus said he was the Son of God, and they didn't believe him. They thought of ways to kill him, but they were frightened of all the people who supported him.

The Last Supper

Jesus and his disciples gathered together to celebrate the feast of the Passover (for details of this feast see page 12). Jesus told them that it would be the last meal he would eat with them, and that one of them was going to turn against him.

As Jesus gave out the bread and passed around the cup of wine, he told the disciples that the bread and wine were symbols of his body and blood. He asked them to remember him by eating bread and drinking wine together in the future.

Jesus prays

During the night, Jesus went to a quiet garden at Gethsemane, so that he could pray. He knew what was going to happen to him, and he was feeling very nervous.

Jesus is seized

Just after Jesus had prayed, a crowd of people appeared. One of the disciples, called Judas Iscariot, led the way. Jesus's enemies had paid Judas thirty silver coins to tell them where they could seize Jesus secretly. Some soldiers then took hold of him and led him away. Afterward, Judas realized what a terrible thing he had done, and he killed himself.

Jesus is crucified

Father, forgive them.

Jesus was sentenced to death by the Jewish high court and taken to the Roman governor, Pontius Pilate. The chief priests and other people demanded that Jesus should be crucified because he said he was the Son of God. They shouted so much that finally Pilate agreed. They took Jesus to a place called Golgotha and nailed him to a wooden cross. Before he died on the cross, Jesus asked God to forgive the people who had crucified him.

Jesus rises from the dead

After Jesus died, his body was put inside a cave. Three days later some women visited the cave. They found that the stone had been moved and Jesus's body was gone! They saw an angel in the cave, who told them not to be afraid because Jesus had risen from the dead and was alive.

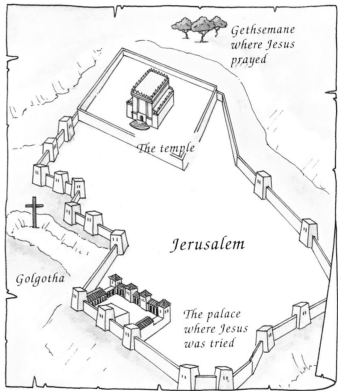

Gethsemane where Jesus prayed

The temple

Jerusalem

Golgotha

The palace where Jesus was tried

The disciples see Jesus

Jesus appeared to the disciples as they were eating together. When they saw the marks of the nails in his hands and feet, they believed it was really Jesus. He told his disciples to go and tell people about God and to heal the sick, just as he had done.

The Christian faith spreads

After Jesus had risen from the dead, he ate and talked with his disciples many times. He told them that God was going to give them the Holy Spirit. The word *spirit* means "breath," so the Holy Spirit is the breath of God as Jesus is the Son of God. After Jesus had made this promise, he went up to join God in heaven. This is called the Ascension.

Pentecost

Pentecost was the Jewish harvest festival when the Jews remembered God giving Moses the Ten Commandments on Mount Sinai. Today, at Pentecost, Christians remember when the Holy Spirit first came.

The Holy Spirit

Not long after Jesus had left them, the disciples met in Jerusalem for the festival of Pentecost. As they prayed together, a sound like a strong wind suddenly filled the house, and what seemed like flames of fire appeared above their heads.

Different languages

The disciples were filled with the Holy Spirit and began to speak languages that they had not known before. Jews from other countries who were also there were amazed as they heard their own language spoken. They listened to the disciples speaking about the wonderful things God had done, and asked one another how this could possibly happen.

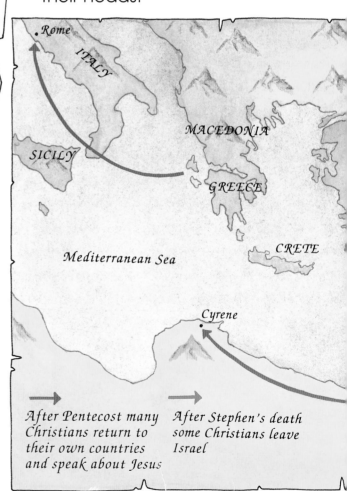

After Pentecost many Christians return to their own countries and speak about Jesus

After Stephen's death some Christians leave Israel

Peter preaches

After this, Peter preached to people in Jerusalem. He told them that God had raised Jesus from the dead. Thousands of people listened to Peter and believed what he said. They were baptized by the disciples and became Christians. When they returned to their own countries, they told people about Jesus.

Christians

Christians are followers of Jesus Christ. They believe that people who follow Jesus are forgiven for all the wrong things they do. They also believe that they will be allowed to live forever with God after they have died.

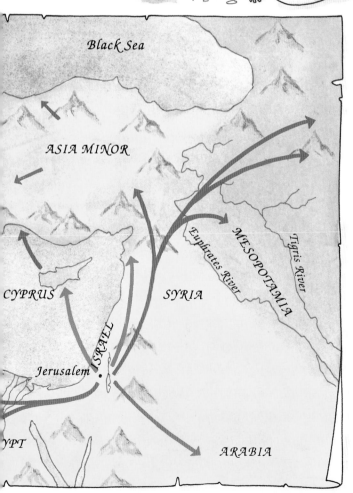

Stephen, the martyr

The Jewish high priests looked for ways to stop people from speaking about Jesus. They seized a powerful Christian speaker called Stephen and wrongly accused him of speaking against God and Moses. Then Stephen's enemies killed him by throwing stones at him. Stephen became the first Christian martyr. A martyr is someone who suffers or dies for what he or she believes in.

31

Index

Published by Zigzag Publishing,
a division of Quadrillion Publishing Ltd., Godalming
Business Centre, Woolsack Way, Godalming,
Surrey GU7 1XW, England.

Consultant: Tim Anderson is an assistant minister at
St. Mary's Church in Reigate, Surrey. Before training for
the Anglican ministry, he was a Senior Editor and
Director with Hodder & Stoughton Publishers in London.

Editor: Philippa Moyle
Managing Editor: Nicola Wright
Production: Zoë Fawcett
Series Concept: Tony Potter

Distributed in the U.S. by SMITHMARK PUBLISHERS
a division of U.S. Media Holdings, Inc.,
115 West 18th Street, New York, NY 10011

Color separations by ScanTrans, Singapore
Printed in Singapore

ISBN: 0-7651-0690-6